My Advice
To Pilgrims

Grant Peeples

MEZCALITA
PRESS

MEZCALITA PRESS, LLC
Norman, Oklahoma

MEZCALITA PRESS, LLC
Norman, Oklahoma

My Advice

To Pilgrims

Table of Contents

The Third Part

The Fourth Part

The Fifth Part

The Last Part

Acknowledgements

Thank you to my gold-star patrons: Richard Smith, Tom Green, Janet Robards, but especially to my father, Jack, who has been my longest, greatest supporter. And there are many others, too, who have supported the records, the art, the poetry, the vision, the intent. You have come to the shows, have hosted shows; you have given me food and shelter along the totally unreasonable path of my improbable career.

Thank you, Donna for all the help with editing. Thank you, Jay Payne, for the art design. And you, Nathan Brown for your vision of this press.

I owe Robinson Jeffers for the book's title, which I chopped off the body of one of his poems, and then mounted to one of my own. And...I am in debt to him for other things, too.

And Ruthi: you are my muse, my heart.

GP

The First Part

Her: "So, what did you do
           today?"

Him: "Well, I finished
           a poem"

Her: "Really? You mean…
           that was your
                whole day?"

Him: "No. Actually, it was
           my whole life"

My Advice to Pilgrims

My advice to pilgrims is…
    tread lightly
be fluent in the languages of silence
show kindness to the least of those
    you meet along the road
and give up your seat on the train
    to the lame and to the blind
    but also
        to the power-hungry Pharisee
            who believes a little comfort
                will ease his monkey mind

Or…just stay-the-hell home!
        —don't go!—
not unless you're willing to meet
        hunger and thirst and loneliness
            with the same reckless abandon
            as a she-wolf
                taking winter on

You see, we can't really make a journey
    when crippled with a vision
instead, we must be willing
    to allow the horizon
        to swallow us whole
So…
    smash your idols against the rocks
    and let the graven image burn
    yes, the very one you worshipped
        with all your heart
            and with all your soul
'cause if you really want to be a pilgrim
    you're gonna have to
        let that shit go

The Lord, God, Speaks in Defense of a Man Whose Name He Will Not Mention

"Remember: there is a little bit of him in every one of you
Indeed, I begat him from your whores of industry and
    commerce, where he was conceived in a womb of
        affluence, and grew in an amniotic sac of indifference
        to those less fortunate than he
Presently, he has evolved into everything I could have ever
    imagined
Here, now, among you
Manifest in fattened flesh
    and hair product

In the Beginning
    I envisioned him the Great Metaphor of the human
        species—
    A burnt-orange emblem mounted on its hood of
        destruction
    And a patron saint for all your tribal afflictions:
        like the compulsive need of enemies and their scalps
        your brooding self-worship
        your incestuous cultural intrigue
        and the paradox of you being able to create a brilliant
        symbol
        but then being unable to distinguish it from what it
        symbolizes

In the print shop…your man sets the type for the
    counterfeiters of history
And on the battlefield…he is the absent platoon leader of
    the jingoists and knee-jerkers: the sock-counters and
    masked torturers who wield your flag
Obsessive, neurotic, fixated, compulsive, irrational, myopic

and sociopathic
I bred him for his bulk, his deformed little hands, his squint
   and contorted lip

And, also, for his taste:
   which is found right there in his profane mouth
Embrace him as the Christ that you so covet
He is yours to be your redeemer, as you see fit
I made him in your own image
Not mine"

A Short Poetic History of Man

First, they discovered fire
Then, invented God to explain it
From that moment forward
    they cooked up convictions
      to armor their hearts
        against the sadnesses
          revealed to them
            through the stars

The wheel would only bring them
    more misery
As did the compass and the sail
With a sharp pencil
    they would unravel
      deep truths from complex numbers
But then bend the math
    like a green sapling
      to accommodate their pathologies
They even made it to the moon
    —and back—
    but continued their desperate grip
    on witchcraft

Only poetry
    could have saved them from their delusions
And, indeed, they embraced it…
    for a while, at least
But allegory is a difficult thing
    for the spiritually incontinent
      to digest
And so, they gave it leave, and moved on:
    a starving herd staggering off
      into the Big Desert

Note to Europe (April 1, 2016)

Softened by decades of living in denial
   —while feasting on goose fat and veal—
      the Continent is now caught in the crossfire
        of demagogues and infidels
And there is blood trickling in the medieval streets
   Again

Because there is always unsettled business
   when business
     is the religion
And the score never really gets settled
   in a tragedy
But this time around
   it will not be a battle of ideologies
     but rather…
       mythologies
So, look out
Gird your loins if you feel so inclined
Rattle your sabers and sing your battle hymns
But soon enough you are going to find
   you just don't have the nerve
     for this one

Jimmy Roche

What do the people want from art, Jimmy asked?
What they want
   is something that's going to soo-othe them, he answered
Yea, soo-oooothe them
Like Darvon on the wall
They are on the hunt for something
   that will match the carpet and the curtains
Something that will fit squarely there
   above the loveseat in the hall
What they have *no* interest in
   is *any*thing
      that has *any* relevance whatsoever
         to the culture
No
Not *these* people
Not *these* generations
Not *this* culture
You're not going to find any kinship
   to cave-wall chronicles
      in their homes
No depictions of great migrations
   or the terror of tribal hunts and
      kills
No finger on the pulse of anything
   living
Nothing essentially relevant to the culture
No eye on any horizon
No ear pressed down upon the tracks
So…who is it, then, that's in charge of art
   these days, Jimmy asked?
I'll tell you who, he answered:
It's architects and interior decorators
That's who

Where the Sirens Wail

The End Times, we feel, have somehow
    caught us by surprise
I'm telling you: it is going to be weird
    from here
        on out

As the sun burns hotter
    —and both flames and tidewaters rise—
        they are going to build their crucifixes
            ever bigger, bolder, and higher
            and demand for them
                an expanded reverence
                and acquiescence

Likewise, from the mosques, cathedrals and temples
    the fangs of diatribe
        will drip yet more ludicrous
            concoctions of intellectual poison
Why, even the Buddha
—with his snarky, laconic smile—
    will sit with a loaded rifle
        resting in his lap

This…this is the future
And it has always been the future
This is how we reconcile ourselves
    to our self-imposed fate—
        setting sails, as it were, for Troy
        then steering the ship toward the rocks
            where the sirens wail

The Fall Cometh

He had been quite proud of the fact
    he had never allowed true love
        to stop him from doing a damn thing
Yeah, pride: that fully-loaded, ambiguous word
And one whose least popular, English definition was:
    a high or inordinate opinion of one's own
    dignity, merit, importance or superiority
A definition which would stalk him like a tiger into his
    own shadows

The real trouble began when he moved to an island
    in a foreign land
    where he stumbled mightily
        with the Spanish understanding of 'pride'
Unlike the English
    in Spanish the denotive cannot hide behind
        clouds of the connotative
Because 'pride,' or 'orgulloso,'
    is not sheltered from the dangers of mirrors
Therefore, the Spanish soul cannot at once be
    both prideful *and* transparent
Which meant that:
    down there in that sultry equatorial malarial land
—where he'd finally staked his shaky claim to manhood—
    pride was purely an irretrievably pejorative thing
Certainly not something to be…proud of
Which was ironic and inconvenient
Though only on his sunburned surface
Because once this revelation about the linguistics of his
    interior had blown-in with a stiff Caribbean breeze
    and bent his branches into swords
    he would never again look up from the trial
        of his ambitions
True love be damned

Is This the End of Getting Laid as We Know It?

It would appear the grand fallout has commenced:
The other shoes are dropping like so much rotting
    fruit
But now, even the hand of an honest man
    dare not reach for a bare knee
        below the hemline
Instead, he hesitates to commence
    with the bold, implicit moves
        required of a perilous hero's quest
            for a first magnificent kiss
His brave lips waver—
    afraid to venture across those inscrutable lines
        of neutral territory
Moreover, eye contact itself seems to be falling into disfavor
The casualty of which is: eye-*conversation*
    —that sweet vernacular, some million years in the making—
        now going the way of drum rhythms
            from prehistoric cultures

I mean, really: what rightful man in his right mind
    will these days hazard a phrase on a sharp, twisted hook
        in a benign overture to lure (or capture)
            —with an ambiguous word—
                his hot heart's desire?

It seems the future must be...Tinder:
That pixilated terminator of woo
Anonymous, unnuanced, artlessly matter-of-fact
Laying all the cards upon the virtual table
So that they may speak plainly...for one's genitals

Is this the dawning of the end of the Age of Seduction?
Is the game changing? Or is the game *over?*
Taking some of life's sweetest poetry with it
To the locker room

High-Octane Generation (for Jimmy Roche)

So-long to the High-Octane Generation
   and all its faulty heirs,
   who at long last—
      having learned to live without Beauty,
      or any of her manifestations—
   can just sit here on this bank of sand
      and watch the river flow...
         black and backwards

Praise now
   the plastic tunes and tooth whiteners,
   the square boxes, the straight liners,
   the lighted paths and hand sanitizers,
   the beige spectrums of knowledge:
      the bumbling, self-righteous light
         we've spit into the very eye of the atom
We, the High-Octane Generation,
   have been weakened
      by a pathological need for power steering,
      air conditioning, fuel injection, solid state ignition
         and push button roadside assistance
            from a revisionist dashboard savior
              with blood in his feline eye

But time was...
   we had our valves ground down, man,
   we had our hearts bored out
We had points and coils and rotors,
   we had bumpers
   and brother
      we had chrome
Back then, we could bleed our brakes,
   advance a spark, torque our heads,
And there was no goddamn "check engine" light

because we checked our engines every day!
We sat with them while they idled,
    listened to their intonations,
    and laid our hands upon the valve covers
        as we breathed the secrets of our hearts
        into their manifolds

Yes, we were masters at backseat acrobatics
    because all that was
        was just humping it up inside a poem
        that we already knew by heart
You see, these machines,
    they were extensions of our understandings
    of all things
    both material and spiritual
And to such an extent that speed and horsepower
    were not just quantitative realities
No, they were allegories
    that fueled our passions, drove our ideals
    and mapped out our interior destinations
        across the crooked fields of
        Time

I have no idea what has happened now
    to this High-Octane Generation,
    why it can no longer burn rubber,
    why it resists lifting the hood to see the power,
        or
        how it has arrived at such a place
            that owning a car that can park itself
                would appear to be
                nothing to be
                ashamed of

November 10, 2016

Hunker down, America
I know you're tired of chewing
But this...
    this is the rest of your damned lives

No, everything is *not* going to be okay
Because that which you have hacked
    from the tethers of reason and compassion
        will not get caught
            and brought back home

Ensconced as you are
    in your zones of comfort
    you have no idea
        just how good
            you've really had it

You have spilt your vitriol
    without authentic purpose
Your rage has found no purchase
    on the narrow ledges
        of safety and civility

Just you wait:
Just wait until the mob
    gets *really* angry
        thirsty, cold and hungry
Just wait and see what takes place
    when the nation's air conditioner
        quits working

Better than My Heart

It is difficult to shoot the rapids
    once you flip your boat
        in the backwash of Buddhist rationalism
    and all the conversations in your head
        begin to steer invariably toward the question:
"What is it, man, that's really real here?"

Perhaps if Romeo had had a morning meditation practice
    he would have lived to the ripe old age of forty-four
    rather than succumbing so early on
        to the call of poison

Just how much nurturing
    —he might have wondered—
    does one cosmically misaligned fellow
        actually need?
Or, in other words:
    How much nurturing can he stand
        before his knees begin to buckle
            and he runs back to dope and the bottle
            again?

Romantic love is not a mystery
No, it's a plague in the Fields of Awakenment
    where the plows grind
        against the cold hard comforts
        of theory

But still...
    one cannot help but wonder:
        "Who am I to think I
            know better than
            my heart?

Petroleum Man

Three and a half billion years after its birth
   this earth was kissed
      on its Siberian lips
         by a meteor the width
            of a daylong dinosaur stroll
Darkness and a deep chill
   quickly stilled the wiggle
      of the gigantic reptiles
      that for eons had lumbered
         over the verdant surface
         of the planet
Cold blooded, they died yet colder
But as the Ages unraveled, their enormous mass converted
   to vast reserves of greasy black fuel
      which today
         —a mere sixty million years later—
         combust fire-hot
            in cold mechanical conveyances
This burn propels around the entirety of the globe
   —and to atmospheres beyond—
      the ape-like decedents
         of the warm-blooded little rodents
         that back-in-the-day
            had watched from the bushes
               as all this Mesozoic drama
               went
                  down

Dear Jackie

I would like to apologize in advance
   for the impoverished words I intend to rend
      with the noble keys of this device:
This manually operated Royal typewriter
   that you were forced to leave behind

It is well documented that my life is up to no good
So, it should come as no surprise
   that I intend to use the typewriter
      to ink heresy against the very omniscient Being
         you worshipped with all your heart
            and with all your soul
   and conspire against the linage of oligarchs
      to which you pledged a faithful and loyal allegiance

But let your spirit rest assured
   that the recipes for soups and casseroles
      which you so carefully typed and filed for posterity
         upon this very same conveyance
   will better stand the test of time
      than my pedantic rants and rails

Yes, those precise weights and measurements
   and portions and temperatures
      you prescribed as a recipe for this life
         are all safe from me, Jackie
They are beyond defilement
And you, Jackie, are forever beyond reproach
   You: who rode a mule to school
   Me: a lost poet, still waiting for the bus

Daze of Reckoning

The only thing the poet need fear
    is the day he will no longer have any interest
      in what he himself
         has to say
This will surely kill him
If he's been doing his job

Yes, if he's really a snake-skinner
And not just some bubble-blower
And he wakes up and his coffee's cold...
    he's in unfathomably deep trouble

You see: the entirety of his private mythology
    is a construction: an attempt
      to gird his loins
        against this eventuality
All his swagger is stylistically composed
    to thwart it
And every mantra and every self-imposed statute
    is a brick in the wall
      that he hopes to be able to duck behind

So, when his daze of reckoning comes:
    he will wilt
And we will hear from him no more

In Defense of Anarchy

Tripping over a kitten
    and breaking one's hip
        is not the end
           —but rather the beginning—
        of a story

Chaos is the primordial soup
    which nurses creativity
        back to health

Ashes and shit piles
    are the great nutrients
        of verdant growth

And the best time to pull weeds
    is after a deluge

But don't forget:
    there's no such thing
        as a cozy apocalypse

A Message from My Mirror

What you see here
    —sandwiched between
        what you had for breakfast
        and
        the day you breathe your last
    —is all you've got

So…be cautious
Because what you're seeing
    isn't you as you are
    but you
        backwards and in reverse:
        a refracted spectacle
        a pantomime in chemical
          and cellular transformation

So, don't trust what you're seeing—
    be it beauty or blemish
No, you are never going to nail you down
Not by looking at me, you won't
Instead, you must take leave:
    and abandon me forever
To search elsewhere for your center
For the soul of how you matter

The Second Part

No, I don't believe
    there's some God
        that pulls the strings

But I do believe
    in momentum in the air
And tension in the room

Shoe Clerks Now Rule!

Scuffed loafers and a potato chip paunch
A $9.00 haircut
Chicken nugget lunches
    bought with coupons
        clipped from the Penny Pincher

How many years has it been
    since this man paid a visit
       to the dentist?
What *was* the last book he read?
This soft white man, with a high school diploma
    and one semester of community college
    working 34 hours a week at Discount Footwear
      where a big black bosswoman
        with complex hair extensions
          and long pretty finger nails
            enforces corporate policy
              and writes him up on cold winter mornings
                when his sun-faded Ford Fiesta
                  with the bent bumpers
                    won't start

But today…this matters not
Because it is a new day that has emerged from his darkness
And he is sensing that things
    are going to be different
      now
So, his spine has stiffened
His gait has quickened
Today he feels a flicker of power
    whereas once his hope was bound
He is feeling rescued from his own inertia
Saved from the peril
    of his own confused fate

Poem for Pema

There is a Buddhist nun
   who has written a number of books I have read
     (with unusual attentiveness)
       over the last ten years
Though spiritual, she lacks that ilk of Pollyanna mysticism
   which I find to be…removed from the field of play
     most of us kick balls around in
She is earnest and unaffected, circumspect about
   things like motive and mood
     and how they operate within us
She is existential about what one sees
   when one *really* looks
     at what's there at the end
       of one's dinner fork
And optimistic about the possibility
   of a person being able to
     wake up
     at the mere blink of an eye

She tells the story of a woman she knew who was dying
This woman had been an ambitious go-getter sort, always
   on the move
As she lay dying, she was at first angry about her fate
She was contentious, bitter and resentful
Then, in her final days
   something seismic seemed to shift at her core
She became happy and relaxed, and there was a smile on her
   face
It had taken her an entire lifetime, but she had finally
   awakened
"There's nothing to *want*," she told the people at her bedside
"There's nothing to *do*."

Myth of the Wall

During their darkest hours
   the people have always hidden
      from the sun
   while the despots of history
      have danced jigs
         to the tune
            of their cries
               for law and order
               and their fears of one another

It was early on that human conflict
   birthed the Myth of the Wall
It has since forever been
   a perfect allegory:
   a poem built by slaves
      to be recited in iambic pentameter
         at the sunset of their civilizations
   establishing a bulwark and a barricade
      with liturgic structures and mortars—
         cementing the stones in the imaginary defenses
         of their Maginot lines

Charlottesville

I am encouraged by the blood
    that has begun to trickle in the streets
And the sudden rise and rancor
    of the tender, temperate class
        against the goose-stepping vanguard
            of darkness
I am touched by their teargassed willingness to...
    not just *throw* a punch, but
        to take one on the chin
        to endure the summer's heat
        and the pin cushions of their beliefs

May they continue to defend the rights of ghouls
    to march with their torches in the night
        at the same time they are bitch-slapping them
            in their jackboot tracks
                for doing so

Whence the Brown Shirts came
    they shall always come—
        drumming the same damned drum
And whither they are bound
    to die by injections of their own venoms
On occasion, however...
    a patriot's thumb
        might be called on
            to help press down upon
                the plungers

Big Ideas

He'd always had a lot of Big Ideas
    but it had never occurred to him
        to make any of them any smaller

And so by the time the end rolled around
    he was having to go twice as far
        just to get halfway there—
            there
            at the center
            of a vision
        where his worn-out vocabulary of symbols
            was no longer intelligible
Not even to him
Yes, he had finally reached a point
    where they would no longer serve

It was then the mornings began to resist dawning
    without any resonant birth of hope
And the evenings were nothing he could settle into
    with satisfaction...
        as every little thing he touched
            was marked as collateral damage
            to the event of his birth

White Man's Blues

They know the day is coming—
    when they will not be able to contend
        with the ponderous and unaltered verdicts
            from the voting booths
      when the sheer metrics of shifting populations
        and the births of newly shaded demographics
            will relegate them to the same intrinsic sufferings
              which have befallen minority statuses
                since long before the time of Moses

Ironically, they are disturbed by an ambiguous feeling
    corkscrewing in their hearts: the ambivalent realization
        that it would be only fair and fully justified
            if harsh judgements from this newly risen majority
            were lorded over them in the very way
                that they themselves have connived to lord
              over others for centuries

Lily-white and militant
They watch the game through a shrinking hole in the fence
And wait for the imminent reckoning, the face-to-face
    with the consequences of Freedom's math
They are emboldened by the delusion of their death-grip on
    firearms and religion, an adulterated political ideology
    and a freshly fabricated national mythology

Jeffers

After he'd been dead forty years, someone finally dared
Collect his poems from the rubble. They were found to be
Like old, lost munitions discovered beneath the sea—they
Still had their charge: they were still
    Dangerous.

But few dared to diddle with their triggers
Preferring, rather, a junkpile of harmless epithets
    from which to nail to one literary Cross or another
Jeffers had seen that men would create a God
    so that they might be championed by Him
    that they might be assigned dominion
      over both butterflies and beasts
    and given holy sanction to suck the phalluses
    of progress

Eliot and Pound had somewhat shared his sensibility...
But never his courage
Still, it was them
    rather than he
      who rose into the pantheon
        before which the tender-footed academics
        kneel today

Because...in a search for something real and solid
    Jeffers had turned *away* from words
    and toward rock and stone
    to anchor his views
And he had bent his back and bloodied his hands
    as he built a tower with them on the Pacific shore
Today, the tower is still standing
And will remain so
    beyond such time that poetry is uttered
      from the busted lips of men

Square Roots

It is a crooked method:
   carving one's values
      to fit one's life
   and shrinking the wrapping
      so that the world is small enough
      to feel safe in

Voodoo, witchcraft, magic and sorcery:
   any fool should know the difference
      between these
      and math

Science teaches us:
   the universe
      has no secrets—
         the stories
         the poetry
         the melodies
         the surviving images on cave walls…
           these are the only mysteries
They are our wonders to behold
They belong to nobody's God—
   a lesson that maddens the scorpions
      now nesting in religion

The Cat Poem (part 1)

A neighborhood cat came to my feeder this morning
    and killed a bird;
I shot him dead as he tried to slink back across 10th Avenue
    with it in his teeth;
The terrified neighbors called the police

I waited for them in my front yard
    after laying out the cat and the little chickadee
        —and my Remington 222—
           on the dewy grass
I arranged the three of them
    in a sort of stylistic, ceremonial symmetry
    which I felt befitted both my keen artistic sensibility
      and the boiling intensity
        of my cosmic rage

Still, I sipped my coffee calmly
    as the sirens approached
Joggers and dogwalkers slowed
Neighbors in nightclothes
    watched from their porches
Mothers tried to shield the eyes
    of their terrified
      children;
Typically human:
    all seemed equally repulsed by
    —and, drawn to—
    the admittedly macabre scene

It occurred to me
    that if I were to retrieve a guitar from the house
      and be playing a song when the police got there
        that I might be able to inject some levity
          into a situation on the cusp of requiring it

So…I did
And even had the presence of mind
    to tune the instrument in anticipation
        of the arrival of my audience

When the first squad car pulled up in a screech
    two female police officers emerged with
        the heels of their palms pressed
            down on the pistol butts
                of their still-holstered weapons

It was….a tense moment

But with the capo
    on fret six of the guitar
—and playing in that all-defining key of
        C sharp—
            I began to enthusiastically strum
                the rhythm
                    and sing the chorus
                        of an old cat-lover's classic:

"But the cat came back the very next day,
The cat came back, we thought he was a goner,
The cat came back, he just wouldn't stay away."

To be continued…

WhoreEyesSon (September, 2016)

America:
 I wish upon you
  your Donald Trumps
   —and the flotsam of their tide—
   to clog the scuppers
    where your memories drain
    and drown the rats
     in your rank and wretched hold
Make fast now
  the loose hitch
   that hauls the sail
    that points your bow
    into their wind
Embrace the wicked tempest
  that you dream will cure your drought
Then lick the salty spray of demagoguery
  that dries there on your other cheek
Their likeness is your destiny
Sail on with them
And sink

Left Turn

There are only two kinds of people in this world:
Those who have the know-how and courage
    to make a left turn at a dangerous downtown intersection
And those...
    who don't
Don't be one of those shrunk violets
    who sits there with their blinker flashing
    allowing the green light
        to turn yellow
        and then red
        without making their move

Instead, be that *other* guy:
Be the one who will pull forward into the teaming chaos
    of the center of the intersection
    —right under the light you can no longer see—
Make your two spins on the steering wheel
And then wait
    (one foot mashed on the brake, and the other on the gas)
    for that last speeding car
        to blow by in the opposing lane
Then stomp on it, man!

There's nothing wrong with making a left turn
    after the traffic light turns red...
        if you've fully committed to the turn
            before the light changes
This is a law of our universe
Teach it to your children
Before it's too late

Americana Stooges

They are duck hunting
And Curly's gun
   accidentally goes off
And he shoots a hole
   in the bottom of the boat
Instantly, the appointed vessel
   begins to take on water

"You idiot!" yells Moe

"Hold on! I'll fix it!" screams Larry
He then takes his own gun
   and deliberately fires
     a second hole
       into the boat's bottom
Another geyser of water erupts
   and begins to flood the boat

"What are you *doing*!" Moe cries

"I made another hole!" Larry explains
   "So the water can drain out!"

The Layers of Irony Poem

He put his goddamned hand
  on Abraham Lincoln's Bible
And swore an oath
  (which, notably, the book expressly forbids)
Then, the little cock crowed
  before a scattering of the wet hens
    assembled there in his new front yard

Before day's end, he'd hauled in a bust of Churchill
  to the office of his new reality TV show
This, presumably, was an attempt
  at a spiritual defense
    against the tooth and claw
      that now awaited his inflated
        sense of manliness

Churchill was an indisputably strong leader
An authentic warrior
And a progeny of the machinery
  of the very country
    against which America
      had once revolted for independence
He endorsed the legacy
  of an oligarchical grip on government—
He didn't trust democracy
Not for a minute
Any illusion of it working, he explained
  —with any efficiency or grace—
    could be quickly dispelled by:
"A five-minute conversation with an average voter"

A Buddhist with a Gun Permit

It took time. And wear. But the day finally arrived
when I confessed to myself I could no longer op-
erate the spiritual levers of a broken mythology.
Not with its enshrinement of Man at its center,
and its banishment of God outside the embrace of
Nature. Once unhinged from this archaic cosmol-
ogy, I drifted for a bit. And it got ugly. But before
long I came across the Buddha, in whose conscious-
ness I discovered the smiling acknowledgement of
imminent oblivion, a universe expanding arbitrarily
and chaotically in a comfortable hell-lessness. I at once
seized upon Him like a ship's rail, and settled into the
pursuit of discovering my own tender, courageous heart.

It's gone not-at-all that badly. Really.

Though today, when I meditate, I do so with a 9mm
in my lap, as I contemplate the slogans, koans and epitaphs
of
the
Dharma.

Poem to the South the Day After the Election

It is dawn, the day after the election,
  and all across
    the scraped and neutered gouge
    of the southern landscape
    the Neo-Con bugle call blows
      —in a minor key—
    a worn and weary echo
    to the Dixieland blues

This is the New South:
  where land and labor are still cheap,
  where trailer parks and slum rentals
    breed gun wielding Christian patriots
      to stock the shelves,
      lay the brick,
      unclog the drains,
      pump the septic tanks,
      eviscerate the chickens
        and to serve as brave bullet magnets
        —aka: patsy cannon fodder—
    in the perennial war for oil and Empire

Where once the virgin woodlands stood
    there now grows in rows
    the slash pine fields
    of future 2 x 4s and toilet paper;
Where nary a bird does sing
  and no magnolias blossom
And every spring
    the vanity and hubris of a 'controlled burn'
      blazes in the collective subconscious
        of a teevee induced stupor flavored
          with forty-four ounce Big Gulp drinks
          and fried organ meats

They are living as metaphors to the very dogs
    they have chained in their backyards
They are wildflowers growing along the fringes
    of their holy landfills:
        cemeteries overpopulated with
            the remains of southern history and chivalry,
                pride and legend:
    all that regurgitated myth
        that flavors the sour cud
            now chewed by their ox-like
                sons and daughters

The community choir is singing in a
    bold, saccharine denial of the venereal blisters,
    the tattooed necks, the blackened teeth,
    the Good Will clothes and payday loans;
Granny watching the kids while Mama waits tables
    and Daddy's doing 364 days in the county jail
        for failing to pay child support;
Lips moving as they read
    the tattered pages of *Field and Stream*
        in the urine scented waiting room
        of the Health Department;
And acre upon acre of yard-sales of shit
    stacked on wobbly tables in the park
    while the bail bondsman's smiling face
        surveys it all from his towering billboard
        there by the Burger King

Yes. Choked in history! Soaked in blood!
This is the enduring legacy of the hanging tree
    illiteracy, pyorrhea and pin worm,
        bending over for the plantation class
            or taking it in the gut for their profit

Yes. *This* is what's left
　　after centuries of seduction
　　　　by a dream of redemption
　　　　　　through accumulation and gain
This is the dawn of the newest New South!
　　truck nuts and minimal wage,
　　fast-food obesity and obedience to passion,
　　the number 3,
　　the color red,
　　the scent of China,
　　the sound of the truck not starting
　　　　in the morning...
　　and the feel of farting
　　　　through cheap polyester

We're talking Jesus here
　　the confederate flag,
　　the fear of science,
　　the crime of abortion,
　　the evil notion of Evolution,
　　the sin of queerdom
　　　　and the sanctity and holiness
　　　　of guns:
All the standard bearers and hair triggers,
　　flashpoints in their new iconography,
　　painted like Elvis on black velvet
　　　　and flapping in the breeze
　　　　at the flea market....
　　　　　　as if to herald the imminent
　　　　　　　　coming of their militant Christ
　　　　　　　　and his theocratic state,
　　　　　　and their prayed for end
　　　　　　　　to a God-forsaken
　　　　　　　　　　socialist presidency

Staying Clear of the Stairs

She asks me up for coffee
But I decline
   this time
This time I do not wish to climb
   those stairs
Tonight, I have no heart
   for love

So, I feign sleepiness
   to disguise the fact
      that I just don't feel like
        fucking her
Not tonight
Not with *that* moon
And these shadows
And those echoes of sirens
   howling across
      the red humid hills
      of the city

No, not while there are still
   whirling turbines of sadness
      charging the cloudbanks
      of my memory

No, not...
   tonight

Now, About Regret...

As the years have begun to bubble up through the drains
  I'll be damned if regret hasn't come to light in the trees
    that shade my memory
Because...
  back in the day, I said some things:
  things I'd like to take back now
  even though I know
    no one was ever really listening
These 'things' were mostly just
  careless couplets
  abuses of alliteration
  vague notions I had twisted up and spat out the window
  vocal echoes pitched across an empty gorge
Back then, you see, it was all about displacing an idea
  that lacked currency
And it all seemed innocuous enough because...
  well: there was nothing at stake
In other words: I had no hand on any plow
But now it is apparent that...yes:
  you may sing whatever the hell you want to sing
  but only up to the point
    that you begin to assign some kind
      of value to your breath
Once that happens
  then your soul belongs to memory
Memory: the weary birth mother
  of all regret

To the City Fathers

Let me just say this—
Guys, you've been playing
   with house money all along:
A big country, stolen
The dirt worked, the mines dug
   and the bricks laid
      by slaves and such
Women were chatteled, the great woods leveled
   the natives sequestered, and the vast herds slaughtered
Your big grinder of avarice and enterprise
   chewed up and swallowed both man and land
   then shat out what you claimed
      as progress and profit

This has afforded you the opportunity
   to now strut across miles of bridges
      you had no hand in building
balance your books on the laden backs
      of the ones who did the work
   then vainly profess liberty, God and law
      to be the handmaidens
         of your self-interest
But not so fast, fellas—
   the fact is: yours was always a
      crown-molding-and-marble-counter-top
      type of reality
You: just an American version
   of a pasty Chinaman with an abacus in his lap
   and a ship full of rhinoceros horn
      sailing in to the harbor

The Mullet Poem

When the warm blood
    that squeezes through my veins
        goes still
And whatever purpose
    may have been this life
       has been
And the ashes from my pyre
    are tossed
        to mingle dust and wave again…
I wish the lowly mullet by
To suck into his throat
    the brew
And meld into his oily flesh
    the splendid days
        I stalked him in
           my youth

Above the Entrance of the Academy

Students!
Leave your books at the gate!
And your binary bits and bytes of information, too
These have only served to numb your brains
and cause your souls
to shrink

But don't worry about all that
Let's just try and redirect you from the path of the institution
How about instead:
    You just set your sights on a star
    Locate it, and learn how it moves among its neighbors
    Contemplate its distance in lightyears with the calculus
        of your own temporal existence
    Familiarize yourself with the migrations of birds
    Ponder the extraordinary brilliance of their navigations
    Inquire about what they do to survive
    Plant some seeds, and attend to the forces
        when they begin 'shooting through the green fuses'
    Ponder the poet, and his divine powers to transcend
    Watch a mosquito fill herself with your blood

If you do these things
    I believe you'll begin to rediscover
        the center of you
And that you'll be better
In no time

The Future Tense

He was a master of the future tense:
    when the going got rough
        he could reach forward
            past tomorrow
                with a vision
    get a grip on a new idea
    shape it up
    polish it
    put some spin on it
    make it hum like a tuning fork

This would then become his
    newly conceived destiny: redemption
        rendered from possibility
            impregnated by the seed
                of his powerful imagination
And he would thereby employ it
    to treat the condition
        of his present malady

This was his method
This was his art
This was his salvation
And this would ultimately be his undoing:
    the very thing that would bury him

The Third Part

If you are walking in the woods
    and a rattlesnake crosses your path
    you should give him leave
    so that each of you
    may each pursue
    your own respective ways

But when you find one crawling out
    from beneath your house...
    grab a shovel
    and chop off his head

Oklahoma True

Timothy McVeigh
   didn't die
      for nothing:
But, rather, for his race
   and religion
For his gender
For his polarized politicized convictions;
   and all their dark, afflicted
      affiliations

In a raw fervor of pure nationalism
   —both dystopic *and* utopian—
      he lit the fuse
         that ignited a concussion
            that blew a hole through the heart
            of the state in the nation
               that was (by far)
                  the most beholden
                     to his cryptic vision

And it remains a myth
   that he really died
      by lethal injection

Rule, Britannia!!! – (June 2016)

Britain has now spoken…
  Out of the corners of her mouth
And the stage is now set for the big battle
  Over Disraeli's bones

Empire has been the dream
  Of all her history's contenders:
The Romans came
  With their lead-poisoned neurosis
  And supplanted stone with bronze
Vikings, Danes and Saxons followed
  To burn and plunder
  Then yoke and breed the conquered
The Norman conquest lasted
  Nearly a thousand years
  Once the kingdoms learned
    To feast upon their young

And now, today, we see clearly
  The Battle of Hastings
    Was fought for naught
  As every plebe now entreats
    To be the holder
      Of the crown

Off-Leash

Look!
There's a homeless guy in a ratty old army jacket, standing
   at the corner of Peachtree and Roswell roads at five
   o'clock in the afternoon!
With a dog!
Traffic is zooming all around them. Horns are honking.
Everybody is all uptight and pissed off about their lives.
They are anxious about whether they will get where they're
   going in time to get what it is that they believe belongs
   to them.
And the guy and the dog are just standing there on the curb,
   all calm and patient and unaffected by the chaos.
The guy's smoking a cigarette. And the dog's just right there
   beside him with an old red bandanna around his neck.
But he doesn't have on a leash.
So, there's nothing to keep him from stepping into the traffic
   or running away and leaving this guy.
No, the dog's just staying there at his side, as if given the
   chance to be somewhere else, (like maybe out in the
   suburbs eating organic dog food, sleeping on some rich
   person's couch, running around with the purebreds in the
   fancy dog park and being the pampered pet of some all-
   American family), *that this is still where he'd rather be:* with
   this old homeless guy in the army jacket, trying not
   to get run over together, and not knowing what dumpster
   their next meal is coming from.

Just look at them, would you—
As the light changes and the traffic stops
And they go moseying across the crazy intersection
Right through the seething guts of all that amped-up
   rile and agitation
As calm and content as I, myself, might ever hope to be.

Needles and Threads

I've been quiet for a while, save for a poem or
two. But I've been reading up on how everybody
is feeling, and what everybody is saying about what
is going down. And all I can say is—I sure wish I had
learned to sew.

Because if I had, I'd be stitching right now. Like
that French woman in Dickens' novel. You know:
Madame what's-her-*nom*. The one who knitted
into fabric the names of all the heads that would roll
(literally) once the chickens came home to roost.

Yeah, but I'd be stitching the names on a quilt of all the
individuals, organizations and institutions that I knew
would be drawn and quartered and burned at the stake
(metaphorically), once the picture began to clear, and
the narrative darkened in the popular TV show of the day.

The Sick Animal

I) Man's ascent went
    from the wheel to a moonshot
      in mere microseconds
      of history
But why, then,
    in even less time
      hasn't he made it
        from the spectacle of Judean slavery
        to not amusing himself so
        with televised malice?

II) Man can't grow up because…
    man is too terrified of dying
"Man, the only sick animal," Nietzsche giggled:
    a course and corrupted incarnation of cruelty
      who insists nevertheless
      upon his little hand being held

III) The reign of Christ was brought down
    in Palestine
But so, too, was the Roman pantheon
Now, the Market is the new God in town,
    raining down its fire and gold
Sirens of profits and greedy spirits
    spin through its galaxy
Therein, though having discovered the secrets of
    freeing himself from the very gravity that binds
      his planet into a ball, Man has
      surrendered himself to the rules
        and valuations of the faux science
        of economics

IV) Man's mind is untethered
But his soul is muffled

Come November

One should vote for her
But one should do so
    as one should kill a snake:
    without enthusiasm, emotion,
        bloodlust or grudge
    but as a matter of fact—
    the same way a woman makes bread
    and with such comport
        as would resemble an old sailor
           standing by the ship's rail
           peering toward a dark horizon
               through a din of foul weather

You'll Be Okay if the Check's Okay

He was smug and bespectacled like any good professional
He perused my chart and worked his brow
He feigned interest in my information
Mining pretense for a discussion
    —valued at two hundred and forty dollars an hour—
    about a galaxy of medicines and their indications
       and how they might address
          what he referred to as my...'evaluation'

"Have you ever thought about suicide?" he wondered
"You damn right I have," I answered
"Lately?"
"No, not really. I haven't had the time."
"The time?"
"Yeah, I've been kinda busy"
"Doing what?"
"Well...I'm a singer"

He clicked his pen as if it were the safety on a pistol
And then promptly scribbled something down

"So, you're a musician, then?"
"Well, I write songs. Then I travel 'round and sing them"
"Are you saying that the people...that they actually *listen?*"
"Yeah. I mean, sometimes. Sometimes some are willing."
He almost gasped: *"That-Is-A-Mazing"*
I looked him in the eye: "You ain't fuckin' kidding"

Another click of the pen, then, the drafting of a conclusion
    in the form of a prescription based upon a suspicion
       gleaned from our brief conversation:
That this condition from which I suffered?
What was it that he called it?
Oh, yes. I remember now. It was:
    "Depression caused by my *situation*"

Oh, wow! Wasn't that a revelation!

The Party

Has the time finally come
    for me to mix martinis and have a smoke
        with that screaming baby of paradox and ambiguity
        otherwise known as my tender
           throbbing
             heart?

Could this really be the brink: the reputed edge
    where I have come to bear the restless burn
    and either freak out or settle in
        with my birthright's wash of jumpiness
        and dread?

Shall I hold hands now with regret and despair?
Or maybe even take her to the prom?
Allow loneliness to be my Savior
    and burst the transparent bubble of my being
        with the whispering touch
        of a vulture's feather?

Is this to be the party:
    the party I will throw
    and announce to the entire universe
        that everyone is invited?

Has my improvised life blown over?
Or has the storm just begun?

On Being a Songwriter

First and foremost:
    steer-the-hell-clear of all sentimentality
And if this hard-and-fast rule doesn't make any sense to you
    devote a few years to figuring it out
        before torturing the world with yet another one of
           your goddamn sentimental songs

Nostalgia?
No, nostalgia it is *not quite* the same as sentimentality
But if you go there, you might want to think about dusting-
    it-up with some dog shit to make it easier for others to
    swallow

Beware of l-ooooooooong intros to your songs
The best song outtro is fastidiously abrupt and unadorned
One. Stop. Is. Pretty. Much. All. One. Song. Can. Take.
A brilliant guitar solo isn't going to improve a bad song
Ever

You should cease and desist with this enterprise altogether
    unless you understand in your broken bones
        that words like 'ignite'
          are superior to those like 'burn'

Bear in mind that some words are just not meant to be sung
I submit for example: 'smugness'

You only get to use three 'baby's over the entire course of
    your career...
Period

For God's sake: refrain from ever singing about 'my soul'
Please don't start a song with 'I woke up this morning'
And NEVER, under any circumstances, say 'down on my
    knees'

Do not underestimate (or overuse)
    the power of assonance and alliteration
Know that nothing disappoints
    quite like
        that exact rhyme
          the ears
            hear
              coming

And pay attention to what Springsteen meant
    when he said:
        "I didn't know how to write
          until I learned to write in my father's shoes"

A great leap forward in this whole songwriting endeavor
    will take place the first time you enthusiastically
        scratch out an entire verse you had initially felt
          to be a crowning literary achievement

Until such time
    continue to write with the tip of your tongue
        rather than the tip of your pen

And yes: if a better job comes along....
    by all means...
        seize it

The People Prefer a Tyrant

Benito Mussolini
—the manifestation of his country's soul—
        had to ascend to supreme power
            before *he* could be got rid of
        otherwise he would have just
            niggled on in Rome

But from the high perch of his absolute authority
    he and his mistress would one-day
        hang from their heels
    beaten, gouged and bullet riddled
He had ridden the harsh, invective wave
    of the nation's trepidation
And then: there he swung

His cult of personality
    had briefly prevailed over the balance beam
        of books and ideas
Because the people: Well, they *prefer* a tyrant
As does the Church
Indeed, the Church towed his line
Not on ideological or theological grounds, mind you
But on practical ones: he would not reveal
    the Truth about them
And because the Church knows:
    the people have always killed their Christs
And their tyrants, too
And for the same reasons

Morning Talk

"I had always wondered," she said, "what it would be like
   to sleep with a felon."
She was sitting upright in bed, pillows stacked against the
   headboard, drinking her morning coffee, with a
      newspaper spread across her lap.
But he still clung to sleep, twisted in a fetal curl.
It was early, earlier than any hour he had known in years.
And though he had definitely heard her speak
   he feigned intractability from a private world of dreams.
"Once, in Chicago," she said cheerfully, "I *did* fuck a plaintiff
   lawyer.
He was Jewish, but he wore a cowboy hat and boots.
I think his name was Silverman, or maybe it was Goldman.
Anyhow…it wasn't much to write home about."
She chuckled:
"My girlfriend, Chanelle; she told me that screwing a cowboy
   in Chicago is like eating sushi in Kansas City. Ha!"

He rolled over now in a bit of a snit; pulled the sheet up over
   his head, as if that might block out her talking.
The bed jiggled, and some of her coffee tided over the cup
   lip and onto the newspaper.
She seemed…not to care.
"I'll say this much about you, fella: you *do* have a mighty big
   imagination; even if you couldn't find a clit
      with a map and a flashlight."
She smeared the spilt coffee with her fingertips.
"By the way, were you a bank robber?
If so, it's no wonder you ended up in the penitentiary."

That did it: he tore back the sheets, rolled out of bed
   and stomped toward the bathroom.
She called after him: "There's a blue toothbrush for you
   in the bottom drawer to the right of the sink!" she said.
"It's practically new!"

Low Falutin

I don't have a lot of time to waste
    anymore
The raw materials of my existence
    are being depleted
As the work grows more precise
    (and less substantial)
      I am perpetually slipping away
        from what it is
          I'm doing

It is one thing, you know, to buy in to your own bullshit
And another thing, entirely, to try to sell tickets to it

"So much for allegory, huh?"
    they will say
As they bury me

Mob Rules

There are some things the people
   should not be allowed
     to decide
They cannot be trusted
   with the higher ground
They are motorized
   by their crude passions, and the bloated versions
     of all their childhood traumas, dilemmas
     and delusions
Their hearts are corroded by propaganda
Their livers are corrupted by sugar
Their minds are dulled from always looking
   down

They are, therefore, prone to take a madman
   at his word
So…we must corral them densely
Allow them their media
But avail them a narcotic
Feed them their memories
And by all means…
   keep a big foot
     pressed down hard
       upon their necks

Freight Boat Blues

Once, aboard a rank freight boat tied to the wharf
   in Bluefield, Nicaragua, he had hung a hammock
      in the shade on the aft deck
And in that clanging din of maritime commerce and
   confusion, amid the polyglot barking of needs and orders,
      and the shuffling of chickens, coconuts and children...
      he had drifted off to sleep with a book of Sylvia Plath
      poems opened on his chest
He remembers feeling the day to be the very pinnacle
   of his life's experience
Where and when all his intangibles had coalesced:
   he and his high education
   his calloused hands and strong back
   his newfound knowledge about the sea and seeds
   his pirate-like machete swing
   and that morass of books he had plowed through

Yet, ever since that day of illumination
   he has steered his heart away from this vivid memory
Not because of his fervent disdain
   for nostalgia and sentimentalism
But because when he awoke from his poetic dream
   in the hammock that day
   the ship's lines had been tossed
      and the captain was allowing the tide
         to swing the stern into the channel
And it had seemed certain to him that the shore itself was
   receding
Yes, there at the very height of his powers
   And at a moment in time when his life seemed to be
      coming together in a sort of redeeming clarity
      he had gotten the most basic premise
        about everything
          wrong

I Am No Atheist

I am no atheist
    but men are of little concern to my God
Our far-flung satellites, with their penetrating optics,
    have transmitted back a clear confirmation
        of our insignificance
We can see now: she has billions of bigger galaxies
    with which to contend

For some
    these are unpleasant pills to digest: that the earth
        is not composed of four corners
            etcetera, etcetera
                and ad infinitum
The paleolithic cultures bred into us
    these primitive illusions
And we now seem unable to separate ourselves
    from all the misrepresentations
        enshrined by their naked mind's
            eye

They were so acutely certain
    in their miscalculation
        that they stood there
            at the very center
                of All

And, still, with every new revelation rejecting
    their childish misconception
    men continue
    —ever-more incessantly—
        to try and worm their way back through the facts
            toward the tepid comfort of that ancient delusion

How Loneliness Works

My mama and daddy died in 1917 from the influenza
    —*she told me*—
I was 14 years old at the time
I got sent to Tallahassee to live with my great aunt
She was a humorless widow
    with severe thoughts
But she took me in: it was a little house
    over on Brevard Street
I finished school there at Leon High
It was on Park Avenue in those days
I didn't know a single soul
And I was lonely as hell, I tell you
But you know...
    it prepared me for later on

Sissy-Ass Liberal Dilemma

In the days following the election, she would
    stagger out into public, swaying with a sort of
        ear-ringing vertigo
It felt to her as though she were teetering
    without a handhold
        along a rocky canyon rim
And with every pair of eyes she met
    she wondered: are these pupils
        some of those blinded portals
            now open to a conscience seething
            with victory and oblivion?

As each person passed she would ask herself:
Is *this* one of *those* individuals?
One who recently recklessly reckoned
    with the Devil?
One who sold their daughters
    into Sodom?

For God's sake, she muttered beneath her breath:
Why don't they just go ahead and start wearing
    their fucking armbands?

Death of a Song Man

Having not heard of him in decades
    many were surprised to learn of his death
They had assumed, at least, that there was no way
    he was still performing
But they were wrong
Right up till the end
    he'd played six-night-a-week gigs
        in the dreadful and drab Republican enclave
        of Branson, Missouri
    as well as wobbly stages
        in low-budget, cruise ship ballrooms
    and horrid, one-off nostalgia shows
        for people whose lives
        (back when his songs and image were in vogue)
        had frozen and never thawed
What a shame it was that few knew
        that even though his star had flamed out
            he had carried on with the steady pursuit
            of his passion for song
            while remaining no more unhappy
                than he had ever been
                at his zenith

The Fourth Part

After my show Friday, I was signing a CD at the
   merchandise table.

"I really love your stuff," the woman told me.
   "But you are so angry. I don't know how
      you sleep at night."

"What makes you think I can sleep at night?"
   I asked her.

Scruffy

Like me...
    my little dog is dying
Though I fear
    her time is far more near

Unlike me
    she is not afraid
And her little tail still patters
    when she hears me
      speak her name

Though she struggles to get breath
    she maintains a lighthearted ire
      for the mailman and
        others in uniform
Her ravaged play-toy remains
    between her paws
Gnawed, guarded, loved

I am sobbing
She has sniffed her food curiously
    but without interest
And now sleeps
    with her eyes in a fluttering
      pain-wrenched squint

But I know she does not suffer
Because she does not resist

Change of Plan

The world is a damn mess
And he's just figured out he can't do anything about it
He's been grinding his gears for years
    trying to change how things are
But now he's done with all that
Why, just the other day he saw a fat woman with black teeth
    in an electric cart
        creeping down the ice cream aisle of the Walmart
She was wearing a hat that said: 'Make America Great Again'
He wanted to say to her:
"Really? You. Poor. Stupid. Bitch.
Don't you realize they'd like to gas your mashed ass
    then heave your carcass into the ovens
        faster than you can say
            'chocolate marble swirl, just $2.99 a gallon?'"
But he didn't
Because he doesn't want to engage anymore
No, he's done with all of that now
No more trying to reason with the people
    or trying to insert any clarity into any situation
And no more trying to build songs and poems
    that kick the shins of the culture, either
Nope
I mean: THIS culture?
Was he fucking crazy?
What a waste of time
He sees now there's nothing wrong with this culture
    that smoking a bunch of weed and watching a hundred
        hours of Netflix won't make him not worry about
            any more

Bear Hunt

Florida just had its first state sanctioned bear hunt since 1972
Cases of cans of stupid had to be opened for this to happen
But pretty much anyone who had ever wiped their ass
    with a science test
        joined the fervent posse to cock-and-load
We're talking pen-stripe Republicans, here
    still genuflecting before icons of Ronald Reagan
As well as camouflaged NASCAR grammarians
    slamming a Bible with one fist
        and squeezing a Mountain Dew in the other

The Governor himself was confused into thinking
    that the hunt had something to do
        with both the 2nd Amendment
            and minimum wage jobs at the JiffyMart
And so, it was he who ultimately carried
    the ad hoc banner into the piney woods
Well, excuse me…not actually *into* the woods, mind you
What with that tremulous tree phobia of his
And his prevailing allergy to The People
No, the polls that were conducted
    while the issue boiled in his legislative cesspool
        showed that 78 percent of the public
            was *against* the bear hunt
But it was approved, regardless
Because this is how a democracy works
When it isn't working

And in the end, it was not a battle of ideologies that raged
But a dribbling pissing match between broken mythologies
On the one hand, you had the so-called liberals—
These folks have no idea into which end of the barrel
    one loads a bullet anymore

All the Adderall in the world won't bring into focus for them
    the picture of their decline
They munch on feed lot cattle served at McDonald's
    without feeling any nausea at all
  But then they wretch at the sight of a little bear cub
    with a bullet in its head
It is the cognitive disconnect here that makes them so wiggy
Not to mention disingenuous
Which is the seedbed of their psychological subjugation
    to those with vastly lesser IQs
Liberals haven't won a bar fight since the birth of television
And, so, in the end, the only thing they ended up doing
    for the poor beleaguered bears
        was whine like little kittens

Then, on the other hand, you had the rightwing Christian
    conservative neo-slave-owning class
And boy, did they have those whiners' number or *what*
Which is funny, seeing how those guys *suck* at numbers!
They've proven time and time again
    they can't count things like humans or carrier pigeons
    or even read a thermometer
But sensing weakness is an intuitive trait of predators
Even dumb ones
And their nostrils were presently full of it
    though ultimately, they rallied for the bear hunt
        on moral grounds
You know: to keep garbage cans from getting tipped over
    and shit like that
Plus, the blatant non-sequitur that they had a God-given
    right to carry a gun, and that this meant they had
        a God-given right to kill things with it

And God knows…they have only just begun

Fearless Coward

We can understand more clearly the man
    who would want to kill himself
    than we can the birds
        who choose to migrate from
            the richness of our feeders
            to follow their bloodstream routes
                into storms and famines of uncertainty

Because…
how can a man ever hold steady
    when too crippled
        to speak to the earth
        or hear her whispers in his ear?

Living one's life is
    —indeed—
    like heading out to sea
        in a small boat
            that you know
                is going to
                sink
And leaving the shore
    has nothing to do
        with believing
        in anything

Election

It now seems destined
　　to be a contest between
　　　　He and She:
A pair of emblems
　　representing
　　　　separate-but-equal
　　　　　national
　　　　　　pathologies

This is not a drama
Much less a comedy
But rather opposing advertisements
　　for rile and ridicule
　　in a pitched, binary battle
　　　　for the blackened hearts
　　　　and sodden minds
　　　　　　of the American people—
a pair of humorless pies
　　being shoved into the clownface
　　of the country

A Poem Is Just a Song Waiting on a Train

We were in Winslow, Arizona
Standing beside the tracks
    behind La Posada Hotel
    waiting for Ray Wylie Hubbard to arrive
It was a late October night, cold and blustery
My skin was dry; my lips were raw
Syd was wearing a silly knit hat
And she held her little dog in her arms
    to keep her warm

Our conversation there
    had led to me trying to explain to her
        how I had gotten myself lost
            as I navigated the metaphoric channels of syntax
                under sails of rhyme and melody
    and how, therefore
    —these days—
        a poem?
        well, it was just an easier lay for me

"Yeah," Syd said
    as she rubbed her wet nose
        with the wool heel of a gloved hand
"A poem is just a song waiting on a train"

She searched down the tracks
    into the darkness
        for more words
"And what's cool is:
    you don't have to sleep with any drummers
        to be a poet."

Stability

I have always depended upon that certain amount of stability
    afforded me
        when I've had a woman
            in my life

Not stability from the luxuries of having one cook my meals
    but of having her at the ready
    to stab at my plate
    with her fork
    at will

Nor to wash and fold my clothes
    but rather toss them
    underhanded and dirty
    toward the shadows
        of one of my more obscure
            corners

And not...to make love to me
But to simply press her cold foot
    against my own
    in the virgin hours
        of the morning

And least of all do I need her
    to bear the burdens of my scribblings
    or to taste my songs
    or to try and peel any words from any pages
I only wish her to watch with fond, remote indifference
    upon my life's struggle with it all
        while the clocks tick
        and the inks try
            to dry

Mowing Down the Wild Flowers

It is the spring of their autumn
And now, just as the buzz of life beholds them
We are mowing down the wild flowers

Along the roadsides of convention
And in the medians of mediocrity—
     Everywhere the flowers dare to burst and blossom
        in their rapt improbable fashion
     Between the cracks and crevices of sidewalks
        or up through the blistered asphalt...
        the reach of dull-witted blades of reason seek
          to beat the flowers down

On the highways and freeways
In the pathways and byways—
     anywhere they dare to bloom above the planted sod
        to give freely of their nectar—
     the crusade romps against these wanton weeds
Whore children! Bastard progenies of God!
Who mix and twist among themselves without discretion
     or need of human care or cultivation

In stagnant ditches or in dry and rocky washes
     they may volunteer to thrive
To dance in the shadows of lampposts and power wires
And to wave a proud little glory
     that's indifferent to the insults of garbage pitched from
        windows
        or the scent of rot from road kill

The wild flowers insult the cornrows
     ploughed into the manicured minds of the imagination
        that now dreams them level with the grass

The Republicans

Yes, of course: they will bear with him
They will even champion him
    during his bombast and misogyny
        and his socio-pathology
    through his sword rattling
        and boasting and groping
    and despite, even, the self-aggrandizement
           and the elevating of his thin, gold-plated
           brand

They will suck up and be cuckolded
They will kiss his ring
They will openly submit to the insults
    he fires at their refinements
In fact, they will line up to toast him
    and salute his dubious achievements
They will disregard
    his poor taste
    the atrocious manners
    his displays of vulgar behavior
    and even…his seventh-grade grammar
But the whole time they are cheering, smiling and clapping
    they will keep one eye cocked on the DOW, and maintain
        a finger on the pulse of their pregnant investment
        portfolios

And the very minute the escalations of these faux
    constructions begin to crumble
        and their pseudo-metrics crash and tumble…
    the Republicans
        will then then try
           to hang him

Snake in the Bed

She looked up from her tea
   and the New York Times
"The only good snake," she said
   "is a live snake
     curled up in my bed
       to keep me warm"
And I swear:
   her smile was not ironic
"Cause, I bleed lunar, you see
My fate spins
   in the dark orbits
     of the planets
The earth is my mother
But the sun:
   Well, that bitch is my God"
I immediately felt
   that the omelet
     I was making her for breakfast
       lacked a certain authenticity
I had shown her everything I had
   the night before
And that takes a lot out of a man, you know
Presently, I was in a frilly apron
   trying to put the final touches
     on her seduction
   the kitchen filled
     with the sizzle and scent
       of hot coconut oil
"Please don't burn the toast," she said
"But I'll still eat it if you do"

Fast Thinker, Slow Learner

Man was born too soon
He left the womb unfinished
Thus, he was unprepared to face the facts
And he had to suck at a mother's breast
 much longer than his resilient rivals:
 like the rat, the serpent, the crocodile and cockroach

The catastrophic event of his birth
 became the germ of his evolutionary trump card:
 the organic, organ complex of
  his highly-developed brain:
  a perpetual, grinding manufactory
   of wheels and fires and gunpowder

His mind became his only defense against
 his dearth of speed and strength
 or his missing fang and claw

It took a million years for him to lose
 the God-like ability to spark a flame
  with sharp calculations
   of bare hand and rock
 and abandon his fire-lit cave
  in favor of a false light
   of faith-based reason

His fingers were to then fumble
Forever more
In the dark
For some sort of switch
 to ignite his misunderstandings

BIG Deal

It has just now begun to dawn on me
    what all the books I've read are about:
Wretchedness is the handmaiden of inspiration
Poetry is born of the steaming cup of misery
    that scalds my lips in the early hours of the morning
And it is my own cultured alloy of fear and arrogance
      that has charmed my life into slavery and submission
        to this tongue-tied storyline I continue to spit out
          about who I think I am
            and why I choose to walk around
              with holes in the soles of my shoes

Why, it was just this evening
    that it occurred to me
      I had never read
        any chapter
          of any book
            that did not in some conceivable way
              speak of things
                that might pertain
              to me

That's my style, you see
Sure, I might not have amounted to much
But I'm the only damn thing
    I ever think about

Academic Smack

Hey, now
I didn't mean to spur your ride
Your stuff's...okay
I guess I just can't help it
    if there's not enough dog in you
        to really hold my gaze
           upon your page

I get that tenure is fertilizer
    for poems about one's cats
And that faculty parking
    is a literary dead end...
    with outstanding benefits

Zip codes are notably revealed in verse
I envision
    your bedroom beige
    your kitchen wallpapered in tweed
    and a stiffly erect red flag
        on a mailbox stuffed with perfumed submissions
           to effete quarterlies

All of this notwithstanding, be informed—
Only losers are users of wine decanters
A politician can hide behind a plow
But not so for a poet
Still, you might try vacationing in the Third World
    for a change
And drinking the water there
And seeing what kind of shit you write about
    then

Poem Written in 2021 (in three parts)

I We drifted here
  as the ill wind
   shifted in
    their favor
  and they became...
   empowered

II Black toothed and dimwitted
 Minimally educated, and otherwise unread
 Shaped sour by a contrived history
 Fattened on the silage of industry
 Eager to leap
  from the frying pan into the coal mines
  from the backwoods to the front lines
   of foreign entanglements
 And to serve
  their white-tablecloth masters:
   the landlords of so-called free enterprise:
   PhD'd, MBA'd, 401k'd

III Christianity is a byproduct of man
  broken by man
 It is not love, but fear, that fuels its engines
 A man strapped by fear does not entreat for freedom
 What he wants
  is a master to obey
  who will tame the Fates
   adjust the cosmos, repair the stars
    and soften the blow of oblivion
 Unable to dis-cover God...
  man creates one from his own stock
 Turns his back on Nature
 Conspires against its divinity
 And worships, instead, at the feet of his own shadow

Final Words

She was dying
And for over a week family and close friends
   had gathered and rotated in solemn shifts
He, however, never really left her side

He attended in capable fashion
—which was wholly uncharacteristic of him—
     to the petty, clerical details and minutia of her departure
   while the doctors and nurses did the high math

Every good mother, of course, wants her son
   to grow up to be a car thief
   or a lawyer who specializes
     in keeping money out of the hands of
      widows and orphans
So, she had never dreamed she would raise an artistic
   offspring:
   a child whose hand had eyes
   a hand that could capture the essence of line and form
     yet struggled to balance a checkbook

On the morning of her final day
   she motioned him closer to her bedside
"May all your art objects be flowers"
   she whispered

Several others heard what she had said
They smiled at what they assumed
   was a sweet and tender farewell

But he knew better

If I Live in the Future, Will I Lose My Memory?

We have now seen the dark in everyone
In everything
Whatever more might be revealed
    will surely leap from the shadows
So, I have considered the raw idea
    of commencing to postdate
        the poems I write: these corrupted versions
          of the silence
            upon which I have endeavored
              —and failed—
            to meditate

Could it be, that like freshly minted coins, the poems
    will accrue more value if left untouched, if they remain
        hidden from the market's crude evaluations?

Might some future generation
    cash them in, as-it-were, for a small reward
    if only I were to shield them now
        from all this madness?

I know they are anachronistic
Like buggy whips being made for Buicks
So, maybe they are best suited to be collected
    for some yet more dystopic future
    rather than presently set for puncture
    and being emptied of my blood

2057

The Fifth Part

Yes, America
This is what happens
When you're too lazy
To pick your own cotton

Mean Streets

I know the streets are meaner and the drugs are better now
But it's also true
    that swagger matters more than it did in earlier years
Things have been boiled down to an illusion of substantial
    irrelevancy
So, there's no telling where the juice went
But it damn sure isn't running through the veins
    of the culture any more
Now…everybody's just reaching
For something

If it's redemption they're after
    they should know it's not enough
        to just suffer
            any more
No, now you must first *carry* the cross
    you're getting nailed to
And what kind of man wants to do *that?*

If they're just bent on finding the Truth
—and are unwilling to just take somebody's word for it—
    then they better be prepared
        for some serious finger slamming
I'm talking about their *own* fingers
    getting smashed in their *own* damn doors

And then, in the end, the only thing they will have learned
—I mean, if they're lucky—
    is that if you manage to get life right
    then, well: you're going to be doing
        some serious dying
            every day you live

The Groove

Clara took a long hard pull on her cigarette
As she exhaled she said to him:
   "You might wanna park that poetry shit
      for a little bit, mister
    And maybe try to get your happy back"
She spoke with firm, lesbian authority
The kind earned by a lifetime of not wearing makeup
Of having never played with dolls

Aside from storytelling and distillery
   she had no truck with artistry
She had never bought in to his rhymes
Instead, their friendship had been born at the corner of a bar
   where a mutual admiration for Jameson surfaced
   and Tom Brady, too
   but also: passionate anti-Republicanism
   and a common, vehement hatred of academia:
      He, and his MFA
      She, and her GED

He sipped the Irish neat, and said:
"Maybe you're right
I once knew this great saxophone player
His name was Jimmy Gram
But the last time I saw Jimmy he was playing bass
I asked him what was up with that
He told me it had become too dangerous
That it just carried him too far out there
But that the bass kept him closer to himself
That it kept him in his groove"

She laughed smoke
Gripped the bar edge tightly with her hands
"You are one crazy motherfucker"

"Yeah," he said, "If only I had learned to play the bass"

The Russians Bear It Away

They are still clever there, in the Kremlin
Though the operative soviet brain trust
—that hybrid ideology
    of savant peasantry
    and idealistic revolutionary—
        has been succeeded now by the swagger
            of a polished-but-thuggish
                math-rich street code

The Cold War taught them
    the folly of a cash-pissing match
        with the bipolar American state
No: they beheld our fervor
    to go for one another's
        throats
And simply seized upon it

Thus, they penetrated us—
    played fast with the process of the US elections:
    secretly sowing discord among the factions
And while they may have favored
    the weaker, vainer, more vulnerable winner
    it was never really a victor they endeavored
        to garner from the fray
    but rather the ensuing consequences
        of a flesh-ripping and blood-letting
            from a pair of mad cur dogs
                slung into a pit

Kitchen Sink Level

"Everything gonna be okay. Really, it is,"
Said my great-great grandfather's slave wench
    to her sobbing young daughter
      on the day he sold her
        to a checkered-pants riverboat rake
      from the great state
      of Mississippi

Being a legacy is a tricky thing, I tell you
We tend to turn toward it in the dark
And away from it in the light

Because if all else fails
—and believe me, it's going to—
    we just want to be able to charm the facts
      into working for us

Because any view we might have
—other than the one right here at kitchen sink level—
    is just armor to make our world seem smaller
And all the easier
    to swallow

Omnipotence on the Ropes

High SAT scores
    make for poor combatants
Upon His wobbly altar
    the seed stock of science and mathematics
        burn
    as mothers raised without fathers
        volunteer their strapping sons

Limp and flaccid swings the sword
    of He who once rained down decree
        with storm
And despite all the damage done
    it would appear He has lost His touch
        with plagues and boils
He seems not big enough
    to look out for Himself
        any more

So, now he calls upon the empty suits
    —with their little flag pins on the lapels—
        to rile the progeny of trailer parks
           and fight the wars against those
               who insult His prophets

Houston Gig

There are two million, two hundred and twenty-six thousand
    people living in the metropolitan area of Houston, Texas
And tonight, a grand total of eleven of them
      submitted their souls to the tortured, petroleum snarl
        of America's most ironic traffic jam
          and came out to hear me sing a few of my songs

I'm thinking their televisions might have been on the blink
Or something

Making music, I have learned, is mostly a physical business
Its pursuit is fueled by a crisis of spiritual relapse
    into the misty bullshit associated with inspiration

I mean, look:
Here I am at the height of my powers
And still, I am patently incapable
    of even scratching or denting the veneer
      of the public's wandering attentions

But in any case, I did the gig, and now I'm driving to Austin
It's 2:30 in the morning
    and I'm jacked up on scorched convenience store coffee
I've got the interior lights on
I'm on cruise control, steering with one knee
    and scratching out a poem on a notepad upon the other
The writing is so illegible
    that if I were to crash and die out here tonight
      not a soul in the world would know what it says
Or means

I just can't help but smile when I imagine
    the value of the performance
      I gave to those eleven people tonight in Houston
        were that to happen

Primary Fears

America is quaking
   In its sleep tonight
The worst imaginable angels
   Of our nature
     Emerge

Fear
   And the thought of comfort's loss
     Are the slimy worm
       With which these politiques
        Have baited their rusty hooks

No, there are no sacred principles in play here
Not in *this* broken-bottle fight
Not with this pandering
   To Neanderthals
But let them all have their day
And just hope as you would
   For bombs to rain down in relief
     Upon the wretched prison camps

They may salt the fields as they wish
Because they, themselves, will soon return to dust
And the fields then
   Will flower again

The Nature of Things

Once again, it seems the day might be sullied
    by my pathetic want of news
I am staring down the driveway
    from my front porch chair
My eyes are fixed on the plastic-wrapped newspaper

It is not as if I don't know
    the shame and cruelties it strives to report
    or its journalistic chorus for all to now rise
        and drink our own bathwater

A pair of mockingbirds flit in the electric wires above
Morning dew is sparkling on the grass
The glass chimes hanging from the eve
    tinkle in the soft breeze
These are all such extraordinary gifts
And they detain me
—from an imminent Adderall-like shot of information—
    just long enough for me to
    drink my coffee down
    embark upon a poem by Harvey Mudd
    and suck in some sacred breaths

But then the proverbial center prophetically does not hold
And I soon step off the porch to fetch the paper

And then…
"So-long" I say
    to spiritual intuition
    and poetry and patience
    and the science of solitude
    and the sense that Nature is grander
        than anything cooked up by men

It is time now for me to chew our cud
Again

Louisiana Bridge

The Atchafalaya Basin Bridge spans some twenty miles of Louisiana swampland. And I'm out here near the bridge's center at three a.m. on a Friday morning, on my way to play in Houston, Texas. I've been driving for 14 hours. I'm weary but wide awake, chewing on a mouth full of gum: that ol' how-to-stay-awake tip I got from a truck driver in Carolina: *You ain't never gonna drop off to sleep*, he told me, *if you're smacking on some bubblegum.* So, I'm smacking. And this masticating commitment to not falling asleep at the wheel on a bridge in Louisiana is now fueled by a chemical concoction of Red Bull and BC powder. Yeah, I'm sitting up straight and cruising pretty good, because this is no place to not pay attention, I tell you. This bridge has a history. There are stories (and they are not pretty) about people who never made it across, people who had to face the fiery consequences of having lost focus out here. So, I got both my hands on the wheel. There's no music playing or anything; I don't *want* any music, I don't need music, I don't even *like* damn music. No, I've learned that music will interrupt my train of thought and make me forget what it is I should be thinking about. And I hate that. So, I'm just listening to the whine of the wheels on the bridge. Got my high beams on. Got my mind on the job at hand. And then...I see the glint of a pair of eyes in my headlights. *What the hell! Some inbred Louisiana-lowlife-Duck-Dynasty sonofabitch has dumped off a poor dog out here on this bridge!* What I'm feeling is not really anger or rage. No, what I'm feeling is panic. Panic, and an uncompromising need to try to save this dog; an immediate, visceral responsibility for his fate, his imperiled life, his dire predicament. He's probably fifty yards in front of me now, trotting toward me, eastward, against traffic, with his tongue hanging out. So now I steer to the opposite rail, hit the brakes hard and come to a stop. I remember that I keep a leash in the glove box, and I quickly grab it. I've got some sardines in the back, too. And I figure I can maybe coax him toward me with the sardines. But what the hell am I going to do with him then? Once I get him in the car? I've got a show in Houston in twelve hours! Wait. I know: I can drop him off at a vet in Houston this morning. Get them to check him out, and hold him till Monday. I can pick him up then, on my way home from Austin. I mean: I already have THREE damn dogs. But I'll just have to work it out. I'm sure the dog (he or she), hasn't been fixed, probably has fleas and worms and all that, and it will cost a fortune to get him healthy. But…what the hell am I supposed to do? I am *not* leaving this dog out here. Sure, he made it this far, but he doesn't have a chance in hell of getting off this bridge alive. If I don't save him, the buzzards will be picking at his bones by noon tomorrow. So, I turn off the car. But I leave the headlights on, and I open the door and get out with the leash in my hand. For some reason I'm surprised by the loud drone of buzz and croak coming from this Louisiana swamp. It gives me…pause. But then I realize the dog is really moving along, and that I don't have time to dig the sardines out of the back of the car. I'll have to just try to catch him, convince him to come to me. So… *Hey there, buddy*, I hear myself say. And I sound pathetic and inauthentic. *Hey buddy, I'm not going to hurt you.* And by now he's really close, and he hasn't changed his pace a bit. I can hear the tickity-tickity-tick of his toenails on the bridge. I can hear him panting. And he doesn't stop or slow down or come toward me or run away or anything. He just goes right by me, like he's on the way to an appointment or something. And he cocks his head a little and looks at me with sort of a grin. And that's when I say to myself out loud: *Well, I be a sonofabitch. It's a damn coyote.*

Reckoning

It is more than clear:
    the planet needs a good wallop from an asteroid
        to save it from the death-grip
            of humanity

The world-redeemers have shit in the well
We now teeter on the cusp of Dear God
    while they hallucinate
        from an ingestion
            of Bad Faith

Poetry, good looks, and an aptitude for numbers
    hide all sorts of molecular ills
But this beast has gone flat blind
And yet…it is still directing traffic

Yes, once you turn your selves
    into a teeming culture of consumers
    what you get
        is a band of marauding customers
          who think they're always right

Arguing with Poetry

You cannot argue with a poem
    any more than you can argue
        with the color of the sky
A poem is neither true nor false
It's not an opinion;
    it's a poem, goddamnit
It's not something
    with which you may agree…
    or disagree
You cannot *believe* a poem
And you cannot *not* believe it
You can only believe
    in it
Or *not* believe in it

And if you *don't* believe in it
    you may arrest the poet
        and torture him
Or string him up
    and cut his balls off
Or maybe burn the sonofabitch
    at the stake

I mean…if he's any good

Having Failed to Have Reasoned
    with My Caesar

I am pleased that finally
    —before I gouged out my eyes—
        I came to understand
            that it's not just me
But that we're all afflicted
That we all walk with a limp that is specific
    to our individual paths
We each speak with an impediment
    that has become our dialect
And we all have difficulty hearing what we don't believe
    and seeing those things we'd rather not be true

But understanding all this has caused me to wonder:
Where would I be sitting right now
    if I had managed to come to it
        earlier on
    and had not always tried so damn hard to
        make my life bigger
        to turn it up louder
        to paint it red
        and hit it over the fence

Chet Baker

He'd had his mouth busted and his teeth knocked out
   in a brawl, years before
It was assumed his impeccable embouchure was ruined
But he got it back, rediscovered his chops, and he learned to
   blow again just as sweet

Then, the Amsterdam police discovered a drug rig
   in his second-floor hotel room
      on the morning that he died
And this news would forever shadow
   the cryptic final narratives about his life:
      narratives which implied the fulfillment of the prophecy
         that any life lived as hard as this man lived his
            would surely end more tragically than most

Indeed, they found him curled like a treble clef
   on the sidewalk below the open window
He was fully clothed, including the scuffed loafers
   so famous for intimidating the tempos of songs

The horn was on the dresser in the room up above
It was still crocodiled in its case
And the fact that it was there at all, rather than lost again
   to pawn, was never mentioned in any of the papers
Though in the days that followed his death
   this would come to mean something to those
      who would eventually be the ones
         who stood closest to the coffin
            during the funeral in California

All sorts of assumptions and speculations
   were made about what had happened
But not one single junkie stood up and explained
   that maybe you'd have to be a junkie
      to know that no junkie would ever try to kill himself
         by leaping from a second story window

Father

You, bold man
You, grand engine of dreams
You, delightful twirler of tales—
    through whose kaleidoscope words
      I have seen the world
      and tasted of it
        like a wet fruit
          between my teeth

You, rightful man
    proud and certain firm
    (and by whom I measure men)
You, too, have been a victim
    of wind and flood
      but have never paled

And through your loins
    I have sprung six foot
      to stand and turn
        and leap forth from your shadow

And there, in your spinning, glowing sphere, bold man
    I have seen and heard
      —I feel certain—
    sufficient truth
      to blaze my path

It's Not the Rock that Makes the Splash

I have stood upon public stages long enough now
    to know how to decipher the giggles and sniffles
    all the muffled whispers and static laughters
    the dry voice of ice that rattles
        in an empty glass

From the molten fires of poetic inference
    I have gathered up in textures of tone
        what goes on out there among you:
            a crowd self-convinced it has paid the price
                of admission
I have therein discovered the Truth behind
    that vague attempt to clear your throat
    as well as the disingenuous antic
        of your hand-covered cough
Because sound, you see, is a peculiar instrument of Nature
Moreover, it is here and *only* here, sandwiched between the
    crust of our gnats-ass little planet and the thin riddled lens
        of its stratosphere, that you could ever physically hear
            a whippoorwill trill his mating call
            or detect a warning bell sounding
                as a poet committed to sing
                    his song
No, the violinist's strings would be muted
    were she to bow them in the hollow space
        upon some moon

You see: it's not the rock that makes the splash
But the water

The Last Part

So, now…the Abyss!

But be assured that history
—the afflicted child of a gang-raped present—
    will one day ask:
        "How could they?
         How could they not
           have seen it coming?"

Author Bio

Grant Peeples spent eleven years on an island off the Miskito Coast of Nicaragua before moving back to his native Florida in 2006. He has since made eleven records, and previously self-published two books of poetry. His work can be seen and purchased at his website: www.grantpeeples.com

MEZCALITA
PRESS

An independent publishing company
dedicated to bringing the printed poetry,
fiction, and non-fiction of musicians who
want to add to the power and reach
of their important voices.

CPSIA information can be obtained
at www.ICGtesting.com
Printed in the USA
FSHW021808250519
58398FS